Elizabeth Shane
Rainbow of Promise

Elizabeth Shane is a mother, poet and author of **Silhouette of a Songbird**, a volunteer within the local community and survivor of childhood sexual abuse.

Rainbow of Promise is Elizabeth's second collection of poems, following the aftermath of speaking out about her experience of familial sexual abuse in her first poetry book. It links past trauma with present difficulties, finding ways to overcome the resulting anxiety, mental health issues and intrusive memories when dealing with her everyday life, that can often feel overwhelming for many survivors. Using determination and passion, Elizabeth draws on the world around her as inspiration for living in the present moment and exploring new opportunities, finding a positive path for her recovery and healing. By empowering herself, Elizabeth empowers others, providing a platform to have a voice and a right to be heard, through creative self-expression.

Elizabeth hopes her poetry will resonate with people coping with their own struggles including trauma, abuse, emotional, psychological, and physical health problems, as well as challenges faced through social adversity. **Rainbow of Promise** has been written to encourage others embarking on their journey, to help give them the strength to find their own value, self-worth and a brighter future.

Also by Elizabeth Shane
Silhouette of a Songbird

Published in 2022 by

U P Publications, St George's House, George St, Huntingdon, Cambridgeshire, PE29 3GH. UK +44 208 133 0123
manager@uppublications.ltd.uk

Copyright © 2021 Elizabeth Shane

Elizabeth Shane has asserted her moral rights under the Copyright, Designs & Patents Act 1988, to be identified as the Author of this Work

All Rights Reserved - No part of this publication may be reproduced or transmitted by any means, electronic, mechanical, photocopy or otherwise, without the prior permission of the author or publisher - except for the purpose of research or editorial use. This is a work of fiction. A catalogue record for this book is available from the British Library. Cover Image Copyright: Quickshooting, Adobe Stock, Licensed Fonts: Caviar Dreams, Arial Rounded, Frutiger 45.

ISBN 13: 978-1-912777-17-4 Soft Cover
ISBN 13: 978-1-912777-64-8 eBook

www.uppbooks.com

Rainbow of Promise

Elizabeth Shane

ACKNOWLEDGEMENTS

Thank you to my family and friends, for their continued support and belief in my work, especially to my husband Dave and son, Noah, who inspire me to embrace life and be the best I can be.

To my drama and singing teachers, counsellor, and life coach. You are my cheerleaders in all that I do. You encourage the change that I seek for myself and others, using poetry to express the trials and tribulations we may face through trauma, abuse, and our daily lives.

For the editing and publishing company, putting my writing into a book of which I am proud.

CONTENTS

Rainbow of Promise	9
Friend or Foe	10
Conversation with a Cloud	11
Am I Alone?	12
The Comfort of Cake	14
Forgotten Mountain	15
Words	16
Wandering	17
A Brave Heart	18
Ownership	19
Wrecking Ball	20
A New Chapter	22
Time	23
Broken Pieces	24
The Gift of Creation	25
Untamed Lioness	26
A Spindle of Lies	27
Roller Coaster Ride	28
Dance with a Daisy	29
The Road	30
Simply Me	32
Pondering	33
The Race	34
Silent Wishes	36
Take a Bite of Fate	37
Unknown Destination	38
Fool	39
A Pocketful of Magic	40
Beyond the Horizon	42
The Unknown Warrior	44
Dance with the Devil	46
Mermaid by the Water	48
Jewel in the Ocean	49
Cloud of Dreams	50
Find Me	52
Delusional Imagination	54
Permission to Speak	55
Life Beyond Words	56
Beguiling Rose	58
Life Without Sound	59
Shimmering Songs of Tomorrow	60
Throwaway Lives	61
Lost Jigsaw	62
Voiceless Faces	64
Frantic Whispers	66
Beyond the Border	67
Humanity	68
Ripple in the Water	70
Echoes of the Past	71
Jumping the Waves	72
Colourless Rose	73

Smile with the Moon	74	Flourishing Your Way	92
Unravelling	75	Sound of the Waves	93
Sounds of Yesterday	76	Puppet Masters in my Mind	94
Reflection in the Water	78	Faces in the Mirror	96
For All Those Times	80	Continue Life	98
Shadows	84	Two Doors Down	99
Listen with a Smile	85	Approval and Acceptance	100
Definition Without Labels	86	Replenished Waterfall	102
If Only they Knew	88	I Stand Strong	103
Fast-Paced World	91	Breaking the Chains	104

Life is not a race to be won,
but there for humanity to take part,
Each step, a journey, your pace.

RAINBOW OF PROMISE

Rainbow of promise, so it's been told,
Colours of hope interwoven with gold,
An illusion of dreams in a picturesque mind,
A place to erase a world left behind,
A life where patterns reflect all they know
In shadows of grey, too scared to show.

Yet sometimes the sky burns crimson in shade
As the storm whips up fury in a frenzied crusade,
The battle goes on as lightning strikes out,
A deluge of fire engulfed without doubt.
Clouds gather strength to unleash all the pain
In a ferocity of wrath set free from the rain.

Rays of new light, iridescent in view,
Bask in the warmth on display just for you.
There is more than one colour for the eye to now see,
A chance to imagine what it is like to be free,
The kaleidoscope encourages the wheel to start turning
In a rainbow of promise, for the world to keep learning.

FRIEND OR FOE

Friend or foe,
A mastermind of disguise.
But surely the wolf is no longer welcome?
The pendulum swings heavy in a troubled mind,
Close the door, switch off the light,
Uninvited guests seek refuge to devour the soul.

Friend or foe,
A trickery of light,
Do not be fooled by the moon's smile with two faces,
A crack in the stone, watch as it crumbles,
Hold on tight to fragments that fall,
Gather them up one by one for they belong to you.

Friend or foe,
The enemy wanders,
Unknown territory or a familiar road,
Do you want to take a chance in the shadows?
Roll the dice, gamble with numbers,

                      Game over?

CONVERSATION WITH A CLOUD

Lying down,
No sound,
Birds haven't noticed, too busy catching worms.
No time to chat,
It's just me, thoughts spinning like a merry go round,
Take a chance, stop the ride

Haven't noticed the dewy grass
Sticking to my dress,
What a mess
This life right now,
Delicate and fragile, easy to snap in the wind;
Do not puff too hard, I might drift too far

So far away from reach,
An impossible dream,
Maybe I'll scream,
Will anyone hear except the clouds?
Watch me as I wither in the blinding sun,
Catch me when I fall

Take a breath,
Inhale the air,
It's not going anywhere.
Slow the train down, no race to finish first,
There's more than one direction when the clock restarts,
Savour the moment of silence.

AM I ALONE?

Alone
Am I?
How can it be?
When the night is awake
And stars dance their magic in a moonlit sky.

Alone
Am I?
How can it be?
As sun-kissed shores invite you to savour the taste of salty air,
Bathe in the warmth of a radiant glow.

Alone
Am I?
How can it be?
When the scent of perfume lingers
As blossoms unfold their heart.

Alone
Am I?
How can it be?
With a tree's embrace lifting each branch with love,
Take courage in the strength from sheltering arms.

Alone
Am I?
How can it be?
Close your eyes, hear the whisper of a breeze
As it sings softly in your ear.

Alone
Am I?
How can it be?
Watch as the clouds chase away the cobwebs,
Make a wish on a seed of a dandelion as it floats off in a dream.

Alone
Am I?
How can it be?
A new dawn awaits in an unspoken promise,
Trust in the guide of an unseen hand.

                    Never alone.

THE COMFORT OF CAKE

A hopeless endeavour
Or ambiguous expectation
Of conversations forthcoming,
Passers-by quicken their pace as they hurry on.

Unnoticed in the pouring rain,
A young girl from the edge of town,
Standing still, watching in hope.
It's easier on the naked eye
To carry on walking,
Yet all she wants is a little chat
Over a cup of tea and a slice of cake.

Heaven on a plate does not pick or choose
Or differentiate between the two.
Share some time,
One piece or two.
Those precious moments linger a lifetime
In a faceless world, too busy to stop and say hello.
The comfort of cake can taste the same if you give it a chance.

FORGOTTEN MOUNTAIN

Behind the glory of a forgotten mountain
Lies many tales of stories untold,
A band of brave wanderers, who have been lost,
Adventurous journeys still to unfold.

Ears listen out on a mountain so high
For the sound of a song yet to begin,
With eyes that witness each life passing through,
Capture the magic of the soul deep within.

A courageous heart, one of so many
Who enrich the earth with kindness and love,
Unknown to others, a quiet voice whispers,
It is not without notice from skies up above.

It might seem a weary and tiresome climb
To continue a familiar path to the top,
But the view will evolve an ever-changing landscape;
A time to pause, reflect and re-stock.

There is joy to be had, as hard as might be
To see a path through in the cold light of day,
A horizon shimmering hope in the distance
When lost hands join forces showing the way.

WORDS

A gathering of letters scrambled together,
Sometimes so small and simple, but yield immense force.
Through spoken verse or written down,
The power of prayer or an operatic song,
An emotional plea floating through time,
It is hard to select which words still belong.

A persuasive note whistled in tune, enticing a captivated audience,
Surely, songs of the heart can soften edges,
A resonance of colour to fill in the shadows.
Be wary of ones standing guard, ready to pounce on those unaware,
A fight to protect damage from words
When a calamity of feelings is thrown through the air.

With a stab of a bee sting, a thorn from a rose,
Lashings of unspoken dismay,
Wipe away the wound of a crimson tide
In exchange to heal a broken layer.
A voice woven in a web of silence
Ready to dismantle and speak out in prayer.

Take heed from the sound, for it resonates in truth,
A rightful place to exist in the world
Where words are tossed aside like a rag doll,
Meaningless and disregarded, lost in the dust of a swirling storm.
But the moment is here, arise and be loud!
The time has come, for letters to re-form.

WANDERING

Maybe it's time to go 'a wandering'. Dissipate in a swirling mist of a cloud and fill it with raindrops. There is no hurry. Wait until the rain stops falling to walk gently through.

The waves are calling. Be lost in the magic of a shimmering ocean. Sail on by until the mermaids call you to play in the depths of a hidden world.

Perhaps it is time to sit on the edge of a volcano and watch as callous hands vanquish flames to flicker inside, forced into a silent fury underground. Nature will release when it is ready to strike back.

Drift uphill. Do not fret if the gates are closed, for there are many paths to take on an unplanned journey. Make it simple, do not pick or choose, close your eyes and trust in the feet that carry you beyond the way. No need to follow the road down, the mist will clear when it is safe for the sun to rise.

The moon knows your name. It would be wrong not to pay a visit and ride on a shooting star. Go far and float high, do not be scared if you sink. Two faces of the moon can see both edges of a sword and not blink from the wounds of a pierced heart.

Find the edge of a rainbow. Do not be afraid to search for a pot of gold, for there is no end in a colourful world. Treasures so pure are not forgotten or erased from sight, no matter how deep they are buried. Find an avenue to soothe your soul, there are always signposts to help your way back from wandering.

A BRAVE HEART

Do not be afraid to make a sound,
Shadows may strike in the stillness of night
But do not interpret silence as the weakest link in a chain,
Forces gather strength in a rested soul.

Reach out
Make a noise
Be heard!
A brave heart needs no permission to beat in a pounding chest.

Why now, you may ask?
Why not then?
Only when you tear away from the eyes of a hypnotic gaze,
Can the mist clear from a blackened window.

Take a bite of a rosy, red apple,
Poison will no longer seep through your veins.
Taste the truth of crimson, daring and bold,
An aphrodisiac of mind, enticing, yet sweet.

See how far a dream can travel
In an open road that knows no bounds,
Set the world on fire in a blaze of glory,
Destination not required.

OWNERSHIP

Do I own the sun as I bask in the rays of its love?

Do the clouds belong to me each time they cleanse my sorrow and wash away the pain?

Should I mark my name on the mountain that encourages my weary feet to take one more step to freedom?

Are the waves thrashing around, waiting just for me, to unleash an insatiable beast, screaming in a devoured mind?

Has the moon waited up so I can beg the darkness to fill up the sky with dancing stars?

Are my needs greater as I take first place amongst the fledgling seeds crying out in thirst, for relief from an unforgiving hand?

Have I the right to sacrifice the trees holding out an olive branch, despite their hidden cover being stripped away?

Why is it okay to rip the dawn of a new horizon before the day has a chance to begin?

There is no ownership, not of land or sky, or of body and soul.

Be humble in the air you breathe, for it is a gift, not a promise.

WRECKING BALL

Life's a wrecking ball
Right now
This moment
This minute
This time
Today.
Lights switched off
Shutters down
Fragmented light gone.

Off she goes,
A figure in the wind blowing along
With bits of discarded rubbish at her feet,
Yesterday's story, ripped to shreds.
Who cares what it said?
Forgotten, crumpled up like old news,
New words come and go,
Perhaps more interesting,
Maybe? Who knows?

Life's a wrecking ball
Currently
Destroyed
Ruined
Laying in tatters on the floor.
Look around,
The wall has crumbled,
Chunks missing,
Where are the pieces?
Can life reassemble once broken?
How can you repair fragility that is already torn?

So many questions, who to ask?
Starting over
Where to begin?
A lonely figure standing amid chaos,
Swirling round over her head.

Time has come
Right now
This minute
This moment
Today.
Stop the noise of the wrecking ball.

Tomorrow will come
A new minute
Another moment
A different day.

A NEW CHAPTER

A crooked path
Around the bend,
Not sure where is the journey's end.
Ambling on by,
Water's glistening,
Stop your noise, the trees are listening.

Should you share
Or shed a tear,
Who is around to calm your fear?
An anxious heart
Engraved in stone,
Painful memories of time alone.

A revisit perhaps?
Time to look,
Rewrite the chapters for a different book.
Who owns the right?
A betrayal of trust,
Truth has been spoken, is it fair or unjust?

It is your life now
Explanation not required,
A shift of power, new strength acquired.
Awaken your soul
With an animated voice,
It is never too late to sing and rejoice.

TIME

Are we beholden by time standing still?
When life ebbs and flows
A transitional phase wandering through
Capturing a glimpse here and there.
Do we wait with never-ending patience
Or ride on a relentless wave, pushing against the tide?

There's no escape from the subconscious mind
As it makes idle conversation with clock hands moving on,
One slow minute, then add two,
Hands tethered and bound, fraught with knots and tension,
Waiting for the magic to unravel.

Is it an unforgivable lapse, a flaw in a weak link?
So readily broken, susceptible to damage,
Could it be in haste to predict time beyond?
A sentiment shared by many a traveller passing by.

Is time our enemy or a gift to be treasured?
To restart the day with new-found meaning
Or a continual journey, running on an empty wheel of hope,
Endless energy wasted in burn out?
Use time wisely, it is there when you are ready to choose a friend.

BROKEN PIECES

No wish to examine broken pieces, scattered and discarded,
Easy to forget when no longer whole,
Is this it?
Damaged beyond repair?
Look beyond the fractures of light,
A diamond does not warrant a perfect formation to reflect beauty.

Soft hands gently caress a scratched surface,
They pay no heed to jagged edges of a hardened shell.
Do not fix what is misunderstood but witness a different story yet to be captured,
Acceptance of whole or in part is surely a gift to treasure and keep.
A tale will weave new-found strength to reform, cherished, not crushed,
But worthy of cause.
A tarnished brush is a gateway for an artist's dream,
Ready to paint a prism of truth in colour.

THE GIFT OF CREATION

Humble beginnings, that's how it starts,
Life without blemishes, not torn apart,
No expectations or promises broken,
Innocent dreams before thoughts have awoken.
Imagine time as an embryonic seed in the ground
With nothing but sunshine and moisture around.
Is this enough to nurture growth to a flower
As it sways in the breeze, unaware of its power?

Be aware of the elements nature can bring,
Retract the flowering beauty within,
Danger can disguise in an odious form,
The pretence of charm, caring and warm,
An onerous task of a mountain to climb,
But wisdom will grow, gaining strength all the time.

A shape in the shadows, a familiar sight,
Keep faith, sometimes it takes just a sparkle of light.
To breathe is to live, a joy to behold
In a life often shrouded in secrets untold.
A momentous gift can build on foundations,
One of love and kindness, for all God's creations,
Dispel the myth of flourishing without love,
With a little dose of magic from skies up above.

THE UNTAMED LIONESS

Should the threat of an unknown roar cause panic
amongst the flock,
With a new sound emerging from a tamed lioness?

Defiant or bold?
Challenging or brave?

Is validation required to prove their mighty worth, or does the
presence of a courageous soul carry enough weight to warrant
eternal sleep for disparaging minds?

To mock without thought or to question with kindness?

Do not fear what is often misunderstood.
Listen softly, catch the thought as it floats on by.
It is not a careless whisper in the breeze, but one of clarity.
The road beyond needs no witness but is there to experience
in the glory of an undiscovered horizon.

Without judgement, without doubt.

No longer hide in the darkness of night, but let the heart soar with
the strength of the wind.
The once tamed lioness
Wild or beautiful?

Now untamed and free

A SPINDLE OF LIES

An absence of sound where words stay unspoken,
Shrouded in darkness from a spell not yet broken,
A spindle of lies spinning so fast
With entangled secrets trapped from the past,
Incarnations of magic to keep time at bay,
Weaved of invisible force, bestowed in harm's way.

Do not be fooled by trickery or illusion,
A beguiled attempt; dispel clarity with confusion.
Count the hands that measure the clock,
One second, a minute, an hour; tick tock.
A cog in the wheel now ground to a halt,
Unlocking a curse, for one not at fault.

Lift the veil, look to the sky,
Truth can be seen with the naked eye.
Sound of body, sound of mind,
Seek to shed light on those malevolent and unkind,
Enemies feel threatened without ownership or right,
No longer held captive by an unjustly fight.

Be brave young warrior, march to the beat of your song,
Take place with great pride,
In this world you belong,
Shine in your beauty, integrity, and courage,
Your voice is your power, a gift to acknowledge.

ROLLER COASTER RIDE

Dare you venture to see reality through my eyes
Or have they clouded over in secret dismay?
Remove the filter and step on board the roller coaster!
Not able to disembark?
But watch closely
As you travel through a tunnel of submissive silence,
Darkness of screams.
Do you feel the terror of a captured mind?
This was my roller coaster.

Step off!
Disconfirming voices not required.
No longer will I suffocate from oppressive noise.
Look steadfast into the eye of the storm,
I will be the one to last the ride!

DANCE WITH A DAISY

Silent feet twirl around in a lush green meadow,
Unbroken by the morning
Sound of excited chatter in the hedgerows.
Daisies in her hair, daisies everywhere,
Fragile strands bound together, arm in arm,
Waiting to dance with a daisy

Spin faster and faster
Until the dandelion breeze can no longer catch you,
Liberating and free
Take a moment,
Pause for breath,
Savour new life from the kiss of a dewdrop,
An embodiment of magic,
Replenishment for a thirsty soul

Find a pillow on a carpet of flowers
And lay your head down.
Her eyes stop running
As she captures the love of the sun's warm heart,
Puffing clouds float on by,
Ready to carry her on a wandering dream,
A gift bestowed in kind, from an outstretched hand,
I will follow you to the end of the rainbow and together,
We will dance with a daisy.

THE ROAD

Am I just a traveller on this road called life?
Passing through
Lots to do.
No way of knowing how long it will be
Until I arrive
On my journey of recovery.
I will get there. I **will** get there.

So many yarns to unravel, some untangled,
Others to unwind,
Be kind.
Who will I meet upon the way
Providing comfort and hope
On my journey of recovery?
I will get there. I **will** get there.

Restoration of mind, peace in thy heart,
My goal,
Replenish the soul.
Quench the thirst from a fountain of knowledge
Gained over time from paths not always chosen
On my journey of recovery.
I will get there. I **will** get there.

An inscription has not been moulded,
My destination,
Or by one's creation.
Do I walk alone, or listen quietly in sound
Graced by the presence of an unseen hand
On my journey of recovery?
I will get there. I **will** get there.

Questions hover on the edge of silence,
Should I ask?
Take off the mask!
Where is the end from where it began?
Is it when the doves are released
On my journey of recovery?
I will get there. I **will** get there.

Weary in feet, yet my body goes forth,
A new sound
Gaining ground.
Discover light under the gaze of darkness,
A shimmering promise in the mist of the night
On my journey of recovery.
I will get there. I **will** get there.

A moment will arise when time pauses to hear,
A powerful voice,
My choice
To change the pace for clock hands to move,
When the past leaves the present, with a future so bright
On my journey of recovery.
I will get there. I **will** get there.

SIMPLY ME

Can I ever be
Simply just me,
Without reason to discuss
Or fanfare and fuss?

Pay no heed to those who may scorn,
Wink at the serpent, concealed in disingenuous form,
A ruse for provocation, words spoken in jest,
In fanciful tongue, yet hard to digest.

Have wisdom of courage, no matter how small,
A voice to be counted, arise and be tall,
Unapologetic for what I've been through,
I am enough, undiluted, and true.

PONDERING

I ponder, I wonder, what is it like to feel calm?
When nightfall begins, causing panic and alarm,
Be quiet in the shadows, ears listen in fear,
Imaginary voices are all I can hear.
Where is the sound, is it here in my bed?
The swirling of noise going round in my head.

I ponder, I wonder, will my mind remain still?
The epitome of darkness, an everlasting wheel,
A tiptoe of footsteps,
Keep breathing,
I'm fine,
Maybe it is best to remain hidden this time.
Try as I must for a pragmatic approach,
An anxious heart is not a subject I broach.

I ponder, I wonder, how to change my perception
From racing thoughts, offering trickery and deception.
Rewire the train track spinning wildly around,
A cognitive awareness needs to be found
With a catalyst of serenity, a gentle caress,
Of air drawn in softly, exhale out the stress.

I ponder, I wonder, does tranquillity exist?
On a road to enlightenment, my path to persist,
A tantalising sweetness, an essence of harmony,
Reach a balance of restoration, awaken the curiosity,
Meander a way through, find a reverie of colour,
Go beyond obscurity of darkness, a journey to discover.

THE RACE

Is there a tattoo emblazoned on my soul?
Pick me on your team,
I will not disappoint.
Am I a badge you will wear with pride,
Or am I the elite with a trophy prize?

A special race for only a select few,
The last fledgling gasping amongst the flourished,
The forgotten one
Adorning a cloak of invisibility.
Wave the magic wand for entry.

Should I brag and boast of merits earned,
Or maybe hush a lullaby and sing myself to sleep?
But surely stars should sparkle in the sky and wave to the moon in brazen jest,
After all, it's not every day there is a shooting star,
Or is there?
A daily occurrence under a moonlit cover,
Streaked with crimson fury.

A continuous strive for improvement
To perfect skills learned over time.
Am I onto a winner?
Unique
Gift-wrapped and ready to own,
Light up the shadows with the glory of your name,
My name,
A permanent echo in the stillness of night.

Confusion
Doubt
Time travels forward,
I never won the race
No gift to bestow,
I am not crowned as your queen,
I was a mere burnt offering
Last to enter, first to be devoured by the devil's lair.

I am lost
Consumed by the fury of the underworld,
A straggler yet again, wading through murkiness,
A place of fractured torment, mocking with shame,
Should I wither in the entity of hell,
Or spend a lifetime locked in chains?

Find the key
Unlock the madness
And clasp my strength on the edge of a lightning bolt,
I have a race to finish,
One just for me.
Destination?
Freedom.

SILENT WISHES

Who do I believe?
The flock, all gathered in white,
Sterile and crisp,
Hidden thoughts penetrating under the starch of a gown,
Watching.

Has enlightenment been shed?
Stripping the layers of a worn-out shell,
Discarded and broken,
Disreputable damage,
Searching for the unknown.

Am I beyond repair?
The clockmaker stops time with one turn,
Too rusty to chime,
No need for a key,
Nothing to unlock at this juncture.

Where do I start?
Scrape the hand painted smile,
A picture-perfect doll.
Witness the flaws beneath the crimson stain,
Time to repaint an artist's illusion.

Should I trust?
Lose my mind to the slaughter of a lamb?
Silent wishes release the dove.
Fly,
I will not surrender again.

TAKE A BITE OF FATE

Is the effort even worth it, does it matter if I try?
In every hopeful step, now wondering if I'll die.
I think I'd turned a corner, winning along the way,
Should I stay silent without interest,
Avoid the ruin of day?
But instead, I dared to peek, look what lies within.
Too late, it's all in tatters, no faith is left to bring.

I dared to dream and wish to be granted a healthy ride,
But my body's let me down, a torturous feeling inside,
The mysterious devil at work, ripping my mind to shreds
Whilst manifesting fear, as I walk the road ahead.
Where is my bravery, I ask? Has it leapt away in fright?
In this journey to be taken, is there an end in sight?
How much more can I endure, of the unknown lying in wait?
Tempestuous ruby red poison, take a bite to seal your fate.

UNKNOWN DESTINATION

Time has run out
Stop asking,
No point to a question,
Same answer
Always.
Who writes the script
For an unknown destination?
A kiss, a promise,
Taste of sweetness and honey
Entice a swaying mind
And capture the innocence of an unblemished flower
Enriched with curiosity,
Ready to savour an explosion of fireworks.
Lights dazzle and confuse,
Bewitched by the hypnotic gaze of a serpent's charm,
Pause.
Time reset,
A new sound,
My voice.
I ask the question,
Different answer
Always.
System reboot,
I write the script
For an unknown destination.

FOOL

And yet again, I am the fool,
Misguided and bedazzled by promises.
Why, oh why, I ask,
Do I pursue a dream of colour
In my own controlled paradise,
When the devil's servants mock in disdain?
Flickering tongues wither the soul
To crumbled black ashes,
Forgotten dust swirling in the wind,
A mere speck, meaningless, in a world
Without trust.

A POCKETFUL OF MAGIC

Footprints take many a road
In times of need
Without knowing why.
When pondering with doubt,
Retrace,
Take comfort,
You are not alone,
Whether near or far
No matter when seasons change,
As the wind blows in ferocious wrath or a wandering breeze.

You know
That moment
When paths cross,
It was chosen
For you.
Did fate play a hand
Or an unseen guide
Sending an angel on your journey?
Could it be
It's their journey too?

When a sparkling star takes on a magical form
And given fairy wings
To nurture and flourish
The voice of calm,
Wisdom shining in the jewel of a golden flower,
Heaven will smile a pocketful of enchantment
For one so honoured
To share the light of their soul
Imprinted in your heart
Forever.

BEYOND THE HORIZON

Take a moment, when the essence of time awaits to transform the hurried wish of a captured mind,

Breathe.

Carve out a name in a cocoon, weave a way through the darkness

And breathe.

Visit the wonder of an artist's landscape, drink the offer from a taste of freedom,

Breathe.

Come sit under the umbrella of a rainbow, be encapsulated by the magic of a fluorescent dream

And breathe.

Colour in the shadows with a shade iridescent in blue, wild cornflowers dotted with soft white washed pillows,

Breathe.

Dance in an array of shooting stardust, a gift of golden promise and scattered kisses

And breathe.

Feel the touch of a feather light whisper, floating softly around a tender heart,

Breathe.

Pause and listen to the sigh of a breeze, a gentle caress on the strands of a silky web

And breathe.

Meander through the crystal maze, sparkling and pure, a place to chase away the rain drops,

Breathe.

Fly on the wings of a butterfly's embrace, savour in the glory of a radiant crown

And breathe.

Take a moment, the moon is ready to guide its shining light, a beacon of hope beyond the horizon,

Breathe.

THE UNKNOWN WARRIOR

Where is the warrior that lies within?
Should they battle forward
Or throw down their shield
And accept?
Is it defeat to stop a raging war?
Offer a token gesture at the enemies' gate
For one is not the sacrificial lamb to the slaughter,
But a worthy opponent.

Heroes come disguised
As conflicting shadows in the stillness of night.
Truth is often hidden in a silent world,
Too scared to select unmute,
Torn between disparity amongst a divided rank,
Guarded
Despised
Unseen to the naked eye,

Yet,
There are some.
With boundaries.
Choice
Freedom
A chance to share an uneven table on cobbled ground,
Dispel the myth knocking quietly on the door,
A rite of passage granted
For those who endeavour to find hope in humanity.

Permission to enter
No longer required,
Do not allow fear of a stranger to block the sun from tomorrow's sky,
Acceptance does not always come at a price
Of a delusional rainbow
Divided no more.
Release the tears imprisoned,
Draw comfort from the hand of an unknown soldier
And walk together,
Side by side.

DANCE WITH THE DEVIL

I run, yet my feet stay rooted,
Tree branches weaving tightly as they snake their way up through my body,
A merciless serpent hissing and swaying as it mocks my still form
Pinned
Suffocated
Into a silent scream.

Who is the forbidden creature taunting with the smile of the devil?
Torn leaves intertwine in my hair, on my skin,
Blacked out innocent colour stripped of sunlight,
Rip the song from my lips,
The laughter from my heart.
Empty mirrors reflect soulless eyes
Out
Out
Get out,
Out of my head,
Out of mind.

Set free my demons writhing my body with mocking torture.
You have snatched my breath,
Smothered me in crumbled ashes to relive another day,
The same dream
Over and over
Again.
I hate you
I despise you
I loathe you
And still, I love you.

Crave and desire the devil,
Will I always be bound by honour,
Enslaved by misplaced loyalty,
Until I wait for the angels to beckon me above,
Or shall I dance with the devil in shameful disdain?
Set me free
I beg
I plea
In silence
Until my voice gathers force in number
To cut down your branches
Forever.

MERMAID BY THE WATER

Glistening water
Shimmering awash with salty tears of a mermaid
As her heart pours into the crystal magic of a sapphire ocean
Mystical and wild,
Yet loving waves dance around her quiet beauty
Loosening the chains that bound so tight,
A gentle breeze to blow away the doubt.
Shadows drift on to a different world
Unable to grasp hold in a sun-kissed horizon,
Hear sounds of calm from an unspoken promise
Within reach,
Waiting,
Softly, softly,
It is here

Lay down your weary soul and breathe in a healing embrace,
A new spirit for a different journey,
One filled with passion and courage.
Lapping waves will guide,
Starlight skies to enhance and shine,
Do not be scared to trust the moon at night
Or a kaleidoscope of wonder at the end of a rainbow,
The unseen mysteries of the universe are here to protect the
Fragility of a mermaid,
Emerge and rise with the waves that carry you forward
To touch the heavens with your light.

JEWEL IN THE OCEAN

Jewel in the ocean
I have found you,
Life
Goodness
Purity
Enrichment for my soul,
A continuous force of power

Jewel in the ocean
A sigh in the mist of a gentle breeze,
Clarity
Forgiveness
Freedom
Gateway to slow down a clockwork mind,
I give my heart completely,
Open to a salty kiss,
Savour the moment of magic

Jewel in the ocean
A prism of beholden beauty,
Come
Be still
Breathe
Bask your face to the glory of the sun,
Let the waves say hello to your feet,
Pull up a chair and stay a while,
Together we will get to know each other
As friends of this earth

CLOUD OF DREAMS

Is it time
To fly
Away to the unknown?
A place where endless noise from a ticking clock ceases to exist,
Embraced by golden sands,
The warmth of the sun smiling forever,
Opulent in its beauty of vivacious colour,
Awash with shades of cornflower and crisp linen white.
Tiptoe in a cloud of dreams,
Which one will be chosen?
Fall into a slumber of unbroken promise
Where time is yours to do as you wish
Without shadows of doubt
Or whispers of uncertainty softly calling,
Just a gentle puff of kindness dotted around.

A reminder
For when the impossible becomes unthinkable,
Of memories past of a captured mind.
Surrender?
Indeed! A monumental task of one who may question validity.
Is there ever an escape from silence to sound?
With breath there is life, the essence of growth in an ever-changing landscape.
Your moment
Is here
Right now.
Relinquish your fears,
When raindrops no longer fall
We will hold on together,
Ready to fly home.

FIND ME

Missing?
Since entry into this life.
Past?
Present?
Future?
Blacked out canvas
With splashes of colour that simply stain,
Then wash away in a deluge of rain.

Missing?
Where are you?
Buried deep beneath a mountain so high,
Trapped,
Immersed in a continual spinning web,
Woven in layer upon layer of tangible threads,
Blacked out lines
Pervasive of light wielding a path to break an invisible barrier,
Shine a dispersive prism on a delusional rainbow.
Iridescent blindness?

Missing?
Are you meant to be
Ever here?
Freedom to smile
Without consequence,
Forgotten sunrises yet to forgive the shadows of darkness,
A hidden universe forging a transitional journey of stars
Ready to dazzle above,
A guiding force not willing to hide in a cloud.
Missing?
No
Not yet found,
Find me, find myself.

DELUSIONAL IMAGINATION

I am not living in a parallel universe of delusional imagination,
Why don't they understand?
Fear is real
Anxiety is real
Panic is real
Desire to run is real

Where is the softness behind the surgical mask,
Or kindness and care for those who face their nightmare, staring brazen and bold?
The sickening thud in the pits of darkness, waiting to surrender my body to the one wielding the knife,
Ready to inflict pain and undecorated scars to mark territory on my body.
Relinquish control?
I have none
Speak my truth in a quiet whisper to anyone who will listen.
There is no one.

My fear is real
My anxiety is real
My desire to run is real
Say the words quietly,
I am not crazy
I am not mad
I have no choice but to appease my racing mind with promises everything will be okay
Soon.

PERMISSION TO SPEAK

I need not ask
To converse
Or chat,
Engage in conversation
Of evasive mutterings in unspoken word.

I no longer require
Permission
To air a breeze of meandering thoughts out loud,
Speak
In sentence or in harmonious tune.

How dare I! You wonder,
Release the caged bird
To soar above the silence
Without consequence,
Leaving an echo of forced naivety.

Take heed,
Not from a sweet euphonious voice,
But integrity and sound,
A veracious witness
Of many a scorched wing.

Consent,
Solely mine!
Change the direction of a one-way street
To a gateway of choice,
Inhale the intoxication of life.

Your life, our voice, one song.

LIFE BEYOND WORDS

Words once spoken cannot be returned,
Whether asked for or not, a diagnosis is given,
Truth heard in hushed sounds within my head. Dare I say it out
loud or has shame clouded the reflection misted over?
Wipe away the residue, or maybe not?
Perhaps I can pretend time has frozen,
Underneath, everything can remain the same.
Who do I trust?
Perhaps I will board the runaway train.
No return ticket required for an unknown destination.

Yet somehow, I know.
Deep within the core of my soul, no lines need be told,
The story is permanently etched, unwanted carvings, pieces taken,
One day, one month, one year, claiming hostage of mind,
Scrambled thoughts running out of space to hide until now.
With clarity comes fear,
A flickering moment when sense prevails.
Is this what it means to lose control, lapse of time,
Recurring flashbacks, dreams of the day become reality of night?
On guard young soldier, be ready for battle.

Is this what it feels like when words dance across crisp white lines
of a blacked-out landscape?
Resignation or acceptance?
Defeat or acknowledgement?
Men in white coats tiptoeing around, like dots of clouds passing by,
Hush and be calm,
The first moment, each occasion and every reoccurrence.
It is not a flurry of madness or a clock whizzing rapid hands
around a pounding heart,
Stand down young soldier and fight no more.
Say the words again but louder.
At first it will crush the breath from your chest
As your mouth gasps a ghostly whisper.
Imagination has not fled in shock

This is PTSD.

I will repeat slowly,

This is PTSD.

Complex.
Misunderstood by those in unworn shoes,
A body wants to flee but my eyes hold a steadfast gaze,
No more stigma, no more hiding, no more shame,
My mental illness has been given a name.
Strength comes with knowledge
Knowledge comes with power
Power comes with freedom
Freedom comes with a voice

My voice
Your voice

Our voice
One voice

BEGUILING ROSE

Shh!
Go softly,
Swallow an explosion of fireworks
In the hope they dissipate into a shimmer of a rainbow.
Should you turn away from intoxicating beauty of a rose,
Cloaked in disguise, adorned in layers of ruby red poison,
Sharp jagged edge of thorns ready to tear an unsuspected soul?

Not this time,
I am the flower, bold of colour,
Iridescent in shades of gold.
Do not confuse me with a sigh of a weed
Devoid of life and a straggler amongst others,
Who may consider their emergence mightier than the sword,
I am the one wielding an invisible force.

Shh!
Whisper softly
Across the breeze of a darkened lair,
Join others with lightest of sound,
Watch
As the flame of a blood-red rose is vanquished in withered disdain,
Fear not the glow from a glistening flower as it basks in the smile of a cloud.

LIFE WITHOUT SOUND

I am no activist, a feminist, or of political mind,
But clarity reveals a cruel world at times,
Disparity amongst brothers,
Indifference to each other,
A complexity of injustice with resolution not found.
Where is humanity in a life without sound?

It starts off this way with the first gasp of breath,
Ending the story from the shudder of death,
Yet, what is in-between shaping our mind?
Is it nurture and love teaching us to be kind?
What of those conditioned where opinions are frowned?
Where is humanity in a life without sound?

A patriarchal hierarchy where silence is spoken
In obedience or fear, thoughts scared to be broken,
Education through society, awareness, and knowledge,
A nugget of wisdom, offer hope and encourage.
Is this the way forward; is freedom allowed?
Where is humanity in a life without sound?

We are not here to battle, but can each take a stand,
Progress moves forward if we work hand in hand,
Voices shall be heard. Equal rights to belong.
It is time to amend, come forth and be strong,
It is simply existence if pushed underground.
Where is humanity in a life without sound?

SHIMMERING SONGS OF TOMORROW

At times you need to witness the other side of the moon to see the magical stars highlighting hope in the darkness of night.

An ocean can take a lifetime to cross, but an elixir of potent tears will cleanse the soul to set your spirit free as a bird, soaring up high to the sugar puff clouds.

Find your feet at the start of the mountain. Do not look up, look forward. An impossible rainbow to chase does not always require a pot of gold to be found. Take joy in a kaleidoscope of mesmerising colour at the beginning of your journey.

Sit under the branches of wisdom, sturdy and strong to protect from the wrath of a ferocious breeze. Lay on a bed of soft feathers, inhale the gentle breath of a warm summer's caress.

Listen carefully. Hear the sweet tune from an iridescent smile of the future where your heart will glow from shimmering songs of tomorrow.

A path of choice, a different gateway, your horizon.

THROWAWAY LIVES

Bombarded by quotes of how you should live,
Life is too precious with so much to give,
Flip the coin, is it that simple to do?
A one-sided experience, may not always be true,
Dare you speak out when the coin turns around?
Are you silenced once more with your head below ground?
What of those conditioned to smile out of fear,
Or shroud unspoken word, false statements to hear?

Comments are plentiful from passers-by,
Look beyond tears too weary to cry,
Throwaway guilt, saying life is too short,
Be grateful, forgive, no need for ill thought.
One asks, are they blinkered to what lies ahead
For those fleeing homes or lives filled with dread?

An artist's picture is not painted for perfection,
It is there to take heed, for pause and reflection,
Yet, an unseen battle is not always in war,
Shields of armour are within, hiding courage to roar.
Be kind without condemnation, a more favoured way,
Join forces, be supportive, as we get through each day.

LOST JIGSAW

When do you stop searching
The missing pieces
Of the jigsaw?
Out of sync
Sharpened edges but blurry lines
Displaced pictures
Incomplete stories, haphazard and scattered,
Identities concealed
Until the clock is ready to reset.

Is evidence required before your spirit awakes
Clawing its way back from where it lay hidden?
A puzzle need not display equal parts.
What is at stake
If there are
Cracks in the paper?
Disjointed
Jagged
Yet standing the test of endurance.
Loved
Cherished
Do not wait until the water runs dry before realisation sets in.

Clarity?
It may feel scary
To reshape the sky with only half a moon's smile,
Assemble a new creation,
A beautiful masterpiece,
Fragmented parts shift in victorious display,
A vision of luminous colour shining through
The gaps.
Some pieces may never be found,
Forgive the picture on the box
Of a lost jigsaw.

VOICELESS FACES

Voiceless faces
Who are they?
Do you ever wonder?
The ones fleeing
In the stillness of night
When most are slumbering in soft feathered dreams.

Is it our right?
Should we know?
Ignorance is never bliss.
Those still wandering in displacement
Across barren ground
Devoid of humanity, no bustle of sound,
Is it easier to close our ears to silent screams
From a far distant land?
Boys pretending to be men,
Indoctrinated into blind following of golden promises
Of the last plea of man,
Save my family.
And what of girls forced to be women
Before nature of time has passed?
Women with babies, ripped from their naked breast,
Abandoned lost souls.

Voiceless faces
Each one has a name
Each person a story,
Children of the night,
Someone's child,
A parent
A mother
A sister
A brother.
Today it may be one, who knows what another day will bring.

Voiceless faces
Of yesterday, of today, of the future,
Do we want a lost generation for tomorrow?
Shake your head with disregard or despair,
Power is not always for the mighty or worthy, but the hunters
With blatant shutters closed to hearts of fear.
A road is never straightforward,
Is a path forced or one of choice?
Is it wrong to bestow hope and prayer
For those you cannot heal?
No!
Without hope, there is no change,
A world will continue to spin on its axis.
Every now and then
Pause,
Stop the wheel turning so fast without question,
Life cannot continue to echo with voiceless faces.
Learn from past, educate from yesterday, change for tomorrow,
Each person deserves a chance,
See their faces, hear their voice.

FRANTIC WHISPERS

Quiet!
Listen carefully.
Can you detect a frantic whisper of fluttering leaves
Hanging perilously on
As she walks underneath the shadow of an unforgiving hand?
Blackened thunderclouds gather,
In position to strike lashings of razor-sharp edges
In fury
In fear
In haste
Without question or consequence.

She pays no heed to doubt,
Speculation,
Voices of disbelief,
For she knows
Her truth
Speaks louder
Than the wind and mist who murmur in conspiring undertones.
She ignores petulant sighs of dismay
As she blazes a trail of uncertainty in each footstep,
No longer afraid
Of breaking the sound
Of silence,
For she has spoken.

BEYOND THE BORDER

How dare you clip a raven's wing
So it claps in silent fury,
Steal the breath of a dragon
To extinguish forbidden flames of anguish,
Entrap the beating heart of a butterfly desperate to emerge?
Beware an array of colour seeping past a carefully drawn border.

Pandora's box has opened!
Havoc?
Wrath?
Bewitching enchanting lies?

Or
Passion?
Strength?
Courage?

Reality in hushed tones,
For hope has found a way out.
Eradicate insidious influence from a serpent's tongue
And speak of the unspeakable.
Release starvation of mind,
Shine a light on your story,
Fear not the whisper from a gentle soul,
Truth has awoken.

HUMANITY

From the dawn of time, conflict began
When people divided,
Those with purpose of living a harmonious life
And others with different intention,
Power, destruction, ownership,
Under the guise of
Religion, authority, leadership.

So many cultures, it happens, regardless of race and religion,
Is it all about power, or primarily based on fear?
Is it under the hidden umbrella of a political agenda and greed,
Or deep rooted within?
To rule without humanity
For those who think they are untouchable,
Can we reconcile living in a modern world
When so many are existing,
Suppressed under rules from the dark age
Where the mind baffles to comprehend
The oppression of vulnerable women and children,
Punished just for being female?
Boys growing up with intense hatred with no questions asked.

Despite educating ourselves from atrocities
Of previous wars and conflict, of the dehumanisation
Inflicted on millions of people who suffered,
It continues.
At the merciless hands of so called 'humans';
Not a term generously given, but one where there are no words
left to describe the cowardly acts committed against humanity.
Our hearts wake up to a troubled world,
Our world,
One where we have a right to live
Without fear,
To raise our future generation with kindness and compassion.

There are no easy answers, or quick fast resolution,
Who knows when we reach a point
Where the world has run out of time?
It is not without wonder, a question rises
Of our place in the universe.
One voice may be a small vibration in the ocean, but each sound
cumulates to a tidal wave,
Whilst breath remains in our body, be the ripple in the ocean,
Stand for today,
Live for tomorrow.

RIPPLE IN THE WATER

Is it today
Or long before
When you whispered to the clouds?
Starting slowly,
Unsure
Timid
Like a budding peony ready to blush out of the shadow,
Time paused
For that moment
And then it began.

The ripple in the water,
Energy seeping from life within,
Did you disturb the fish
Swimming around like shimmering glass
In an unrecognisable reflection?
Is it frantic chaos or tranquil calm
As the echoes of your voice
Dare to break the silence of the night?
Each sound
Stronger.

Watch closely as your words swirl round and round,
Bewildering the darkness below
In preparation to carry the storm through the waves,
Douse the fury in the saltwater mist
As you seep into glittering drops of the ocean,
Create a cascade of change,
Embrace the world with your truth.

ECHOES OF THE PAST

Echoes of the past drift and wander
Sometimes a fleeting shadow gently passing by,
Or a ferocious breeze, determined and steadfast,
Ready to squeeze the gasp of breath from your chest.
How loud is the beating drum as it bursts through without care?
Is it permissible to suffocate the noise,
Or feign hope it will roll into the distance?
Perhaps it is time to allow harmonious rapture to engulf.

Echoes of the past drift and wander
Without warning, an unwelcome visitor
Unwilling to reconcile the contradictory voices devouring the light,
Which one will rule
The forbidden flame from yesterday?
Is there ever enough space to allow stories of today
To filter sounds for tomorrow?
Maybe, just maybe, there is.

Echoes of the past drift and wander
Seeping through,
A small babbling brook of careless laughter in surprise,
For a cloud is not always a silhouette in a sunless sky,
But of stillness and calm,
Capturing the golden rays of treasured memories.
Fear not, the eye of the storm
Whether a whirlwind of days past,
Or moments of surrendered uncertainty,
There is no exactness to a new dawn;
Let your mind find peace in who you are today.

JUMPING THE WAVES

No fractures, or stolen moments,
Just golden treasured memories
Jumping over waves,
A story without blemishes,
Not torn or broken,
But simple wonder
Of childhood innocence as they absorb the goodness life has to offer;
Photographic capture, exquisite pain
Of what could have been.
Will the ocean forgive time snatched without sound?

There was no other gateway
For painted pictures frozen still,
Rewrite a new story,
It may be an unfamiliar chapter,
A different path chosen,
But for you to cherish
In the here and now
With simple wonder,
Take a leap of faith
And jump over the waves.

COLOURLESS ROSE

Subtle edges, a mere stab of a pin,
Starting off slowly, then seeping within,
Colourless rose, once luscious and red,
Devoid of its life where blood has been shed,
An illusion of thought swaying with power,
A tempting persuasion for one painful flower,
Sometimes a straggler, gasping for air,
On other occasions, lacking from care.

Is it time to surrender with no sun around,
Withering slowly back into the ground?
Silent fury of whispering despair,
Intentions are fading without hope of a prayer.

Tumbling
Falling
Spiralling down.

Water
Nurture
Replenish the crown.

Hang on little flower, the black fog shall clear,
A gentle blush out of shadow will soon reappear.

SMILE WITH THE MOON

I pause in wonder as the moon winks at me
Under the grace of a starlit sky,
Do you recognise who I am? I ask,
I am not who you think behind the mask.
Gentle clouds softly caress my hair in a loving breeze
As I brush falling raindrops away.

The moon winks again, this time with an encouraging smile,
I continue quietly,
My face,
It hides a smile of hand painted wishes
Out of longing to be woven into fabric of a closed heart,
With remembrance of forbidden, conflicting goodbyes.

I ask,
Why have you not turned away from me
As others have?
Do you not look with downcast eyes in disdainful shame?
Stars gather round, shining brightly without hint of confusion,
Dare I remove the mask for the skies to see?
Will the universe judge if truth reveals shadows of sorrow
On days where the sun forgets to blush
And trees rustle in casual whispers?
Scoop me up into the distance.
Perhaps
In time
On this day each year, I can share my smile with the moon.

UNRAVELLING

Has time lapsed beyond repair
To sever the ties bound so tight?
Thus, a forgotten breath,
So absorbed is she, in the sway of darkness,
Watching over the one who lays in quiet slumber,
Barely a quiver of sound bestows on the young,
Unaware of the weight of forbidden chains.
A familiar scene,
One replayed like a continual spinning ball.

It must be now,
It cannot wait until sunrise breaks
Or when the moon takes a bow in forced persuasion.
Shatter the entity of twisted coercion
And suffer no more.
A guttural roar of deep wrenching pain
Will break the silence with thy wielded axe.

Close your eyes, oh little one,
For she shall clasp your hidden sorrow under golden layers
And cradle you into her warm embrace,
Until dawn is ready to awaken.

SOUNDS OF YESTERDAY

What if I whisper quietly, would you hear me in an ocean's breeze?
Spoken softly
In fear
Of being turned away by the eye of the storm,
Yearning in a puzzled heart
To be the embodiment of goodness,
For truth is captured within my soul,
Not wanting to disturb the soothing ripple of crystal purity
Who embraced, not the fragmented part, but accepted as whole.

Questions,
So many
To pick and choose,
Select one and throw into the sea,
Watch carefully as the tide returns
With clarity
Or confusion?
There is no malice to wish for calmness of a wave,
Or a loving smile from the other side of the moon
Who
I've yet to greet hello.

And still,
Despite continual warmth from the sun,
I feel discarded.
Paper blowing casually around, of forgotten stories,
My story.
Will you notice a mere blot on the landscape,
Or does the sky ask for a hue of chosen colours only?
There will come a time when shadows of grey are wiped out
In rays of iridescent smiles.

My smile,
For me,
For you,
For those still unaware,
Sounds of yesterday, voices for tomorrow.

REFLECTION IN THE WATER

Passing gently through the sand,
A pause is taken at the water's edge.
What ails you, my child? Asks the unknown one.
She looks up, startled by the break in quiet sound,
Where is my reflection in the water?
I hear lapping to and fro of an unhurried wave
Yet,
I see no stillness nor shimmer.
I have travelled far and beyond to find the beginning of the end,
Only, it has vanished
Into blankness of empty time.
Why might it share only murky darkness?
Shadows exist, my child, in forgotten sighs,
Come sit and look forward in to lighter reflection,
For it is there but can hide deep within, until ready to seek.

She gazes again.

My wings, I see damaged and torn,
I see not of the tear, but each strand, a symbol of woven strength.
My eyes, they are empty panes,
Your eyes hold many a story of courage and truth.
My lips are a mere tremble of fear,
Your mouth is no longer a silent whisper,
But a voice of determined bravery,
A beautiful sound to lift and rejoice
As you speak, so too, people shall listen.
But what if my wings are forever clipped?
A flight is not without hesitant wonder,
Look closer, our reflection is interwoven,
Bear witness to a ripple of hope,
I believe and so too will you, my child.

As she lifted her eyes to the glimmer of a new horizon,
Her wings began to open,
Leaving a smile of reflection in the water.

FOR ALL THOSE TIMES

For all those times
You stripped away my layers,
Made me taste forbidden fruit,
Forced my hands to do your work,
Penetrated beyond boundaries,
Hands snaked around my neck ready to silence the sound.

For all those times
I never said no.

For all those times
I endured unwanted shadows creeping inside,
Felt cold metal of a barrelled gun pushed against my head,
Suffered perversion of injustice,
Paralysed my breath through restrained fear,
Offered my services on a plate.

For all those times
I never said no.

For all those times
I quickened my footsteps down a dim lit path,
Criss-crossed patterns in the road to shake away the followers,
Barricaded my sanctuary through blockades of furniture,
Feigned sleep to hasten your desire,
Gave you permission without speaking a word.

For all those times
I never said no.

For all those times
I didn't scream,
Kept quiet,
Stayed silent,
Never fought back,
Ever told.

For all those times
I never said no.

For all those times
I felt special,
Chosen by you,
Thought you loved me,
Wanted your attention,
Asked for more.

For all those times
I never said no.

For all those times
I trusted you,
Loved you,
Despised you,
Feared you,
Missed you.

For all those times
I never said no.

For all those times
I trembled to speak,
Felt ashamed,
Pushed the knife deeper in,
Faded into darkness,
Shattered into broken pieces.

For all those times
I never said no.

For all those times
I am haunted daily,
I speak out.
Fear will no longer silence me,
My voice shall be heard,
Truth will resonate.

For all those times
I never said no.

For all those times
I wasn't asked,
I give myself permission.
My choice
My body
My right.

For all those times
I never said no.

For all those times
I longed to say stop,
Stop!
I am the adult
With ownership
Of my freedom.

For all those times
I never said no.

For all those times
You think you won,
Of lives destroyed.
We will stand strong,
United in power,
Together as one.

For all these times
We will say no.

SHADOWS

If I hold you to the light, would you still be there,
Lingering permeation, doing your best to outstay your welcome?
Tap, tap, tapping.
Always seeking a way to keep me hostage in the dark,
My shadow.

Were we ever friends,
Where I could hide
Under a blackened void of nothingness with you,
On days, not being able to endure withered scorn from the sun
If I dare glimpse the face of brightness?
Once my protector, now my nemesis.
Have you escaped, or will you always hover,
Pretending to be my shelter?

Fade into the background, dear shadow,
For we can no longer be together,
I shall take cover under a different umbrella
With no desire for you to blemish the horizon.
My choice, my decision, my time
To find a spectrum of colour
In the road ahead,
With a new friend called hope.
I bid you adieu my shadow.

LISTEN WITH A SMILE

What is laughter without a smile?
I whispered, as the trees bowed their branches to listen.
You heard me, when throughout far and wide, no one else dared

Until now

When heavens opened their eyes and wept
As I danced freely in the raindrops.
What is my life if it is not for living,
Whether with quiet voice or powerful roar,
Gently easing out of the mist
Or basking boldly in the brightness of warmth?
Whatever I choose, wherever I go, I am no longer alone.

DEFINITION WITHOUT LABELS

What defines courage and bravery?
Is it selfless acts of individuals risking their lives for others
In dangerous conflicts of war
Every day on the front line,
Whether soldier or civilian?

What defines courage and bravery?
A worn-down mother too exhausted to continue,
Yet somehow does,
The one who receives unwelcome news from their doctor
On a day when life seemed rosy before conversation,
Who sees the pain of the young in their hospital bed
As they smile through treatment,
Even though a simple wish to run and play is all they desire?

What defines courage and bravery?
The parent to be, whose loss is insurmountable in unspoken grief
Saying goodbye to a loved one for the last time?
Can it just be waking up, knowing you have survived another day,
Or the one who puts down the knife and says no?

What defines courage and bravery?
Breaking free out of a violent situation,
Being unable to speak of hidden sorrow,
Living in fear, yet somehow showing up,
Standing in a crowd despite knowing your heart will panic?

What defines courage and bravery?
The boy too shy to speak in class, but inside holds a thousand beautiful words?
Is it the person who says they are sorry?
Do you have to climb the highest mountain to bear strength,
Or the one quietly going about their day without anyone ever knowing their story?

What defines courage and bravery?
It is not necessarily death-defying jumps
Or those who speak louder.
It can be soft and gentle, dignified yet determined,
Battles are not always in war and not everything need be a battle.

What defines courage and bravery
Does not require a hand-picked label, compartmentalised into separate boxes,
Each one wearing a sign.
A person faces courage and bravery in many ways,
Life is not a race to be won, but there for humanity to take part,
Each step, a journey, your pace.

IF ONLY THEY KNEW

If only they knew
The other side of the moon
Where darkness struggles to emerge against the dawn of horizon.

If only they knew
The rage of flames
Flickering and tormenting shadows within.

If only they knew
The pretence of charm
Hiding a demon's embrace suffocating any escape.

If only they knew
The tightened grip of a knife
Clenched in fury, ready to strike out.

If only they knew
The shameful disdain of unravelling carefully concealed threads,
So desperately trying to remain intact.

If only they knew
The reflection in the mirror,
Shining bright imperfections, only you can see.

If only they knew
The desire to surrender
When a blemished canvas loses its rainbow of colour.

If only they knew
The secret wishes
Consumed by fear, unable to share.

If only they knew
The blackened thoughts
Ticking loudly in a frozen clock, paralysed in time.

If only they knew
The broken jigsaw,
Waiting for new pieces in hope of repair.

If only they knew
The smile of normality
In a twisted illusion of reality.

If only they knew
The depths of conversation
Spoken softly, in prayer and forgiveness.

If only they knew
The eyes clouded by confusion,
In wonder and question of what lies beyond.

If only they knew
The doubt and resignation
Swimming out of depth, without understanding the ocean's voice.

If only they knew
The colours of gold,
Ready to immerse in iridescent warmth and love.

If only they knew
The sound of your voice
Wavers in honesty and truth.

If only they knew
The sun fades quicker
If you are captured in a hurried cloud.

If only they knew
The journey you take
May often need direction.

If only they knew
The strength and courage
Exists in us all, to look beyond blurred edges and see the light.

If only they knew
The chance for tomorrow
Can only begin with today.

If only they knew.

FAST-PACED WORLD

A fast-paced universe with no spare breath,
Cramming minds full of twenty-four-hour activities,
Rushing here, running there,
Wired like a fast locomotive train, not able to stop,
But how much of it do we notice?

There are moments when time is needed to slow down,
To take stock and reflect the importance of what is around us,
Whether immersed in the glow of sunlight,
Or inhaling the sweet scent of dewy grass,
Fresh from autumn's rain,
Catching up on the book you put aside,
Eating cake, you promised yourself.
Is it so wrong to pause, even for a minute?
Enjoy what you want to do,
Not everything we anticipate need be a task,
We all have moments of monotony,
Whether the daily grind of work
Or the endless cycle of household chores,
Keeping up with little things or expectations
Which at times, feel insurmountable.

Can we say no, or is a road paved with guilt?
Not all decisions are forever.
Be curious with the world around,
For life is an ever-changing landscape,
It moves even when we stand still.
One doesn't need to walk the whole mile
To find new chances along the way.

FLOURISHING YOUR WAY

A flower buds in seasonal rapture,
On occasion it may choose not to bloom,
Protecting delicate petals from harsh elements of nature
Until such time it is ready to peep out into sunshine,
Ready to flourish in all its beauty.

Tree branches bend and break in the howl of an unforgiving storm,
Leaves gather one by one to find shelter,
But firm roots stay behind,
Standing strong in its glory,
Embracing the sanctity of rebirth.

The ocean's voice roars
In crashing warning to merciless rocks,
Waves drift and carry afar a troubled sigh,
Beyond where the sky meets the horizon,
Do not shy away from the shore,
But return home with the tide for a breath-taking ride.

Night time sky does not guarantee the moon winks,
Nor does the sun always shimmer in cloud,
Stars find different ways to sparkle,
Whether they shine today or wait for tomorrow.
Life knows you are there smiling back in readiness for adventure.

SOUND OF THE WAVES

With every angry wave, my heart cries with you,
Deep
Anguished
Pain.
I hear you calling from the depths of yesterday,
Sound of the waves passing through,
Not forgotten

For each gentle loving crest, my heart returns,
Cleansed,
Enlightened,
Empowered,
Uplifted.
The embodiment of tranquillity, calm and healing,
From every drop of the ocean,
Sound of the waves passing through,
Re-emerging with kindness,
Pushing me forward to a new rainbow.

PUPPET MASTERS IN MY MIND

I do my utmost
To fast-forward time
Or make clock hands stop.

I try my best
To find the answer,
Yet my eyes are closed to the question.

I find methods
To eradicate all scenarios,
Only they are puppet masters in my mind.

I search out
A desperate cure
Which has yet to happen.

I look back
In frozen fear
For the day that hasn't started.

I hide away
From crowds of enjoyment
In moments of unseen uncertainty.

Only I know
The sun will shine,
Even if I'm cloaked in darkness.

Night-time falls
Regardless if I long for daylight,
I cannot keep today under lock and key

Because tomorrow will always arrive,
Whether through the roar of a lion or quiet as a mouse,
In shades of grey or kaleidoscope of a rainbow.

I will aim
To breathe.

FACES IN THE MIRROR

If I had rearranged the clouds,
You would have drifted on afar,
A place in sweet surroundings,
To sparkle like a star

But I chose to keep you near
And kept the shutters closed,
With utmost control, to silence
Perpetual fear if you disclosed.

If I had conversed gently to the waves
To accompany you away from shore,
Swimming shyly with the mermaids,
A different life, to discover and explore

Yet I ignored the desperate pleading,
Evaporating mist into the rain.
Who is there to bear witness
If darkness hides shadows of pain?

If I had strength to move the landscape,
Flourishing beauty amongst the flowers
Dancing freely in the raindrops,
Unaware of all your powers

Still, I fought with sunlight rising,
Forbidding any glimpse of light,
Imagine, destruction brewing
If permission granted your right.

If I had listened to the heavens,
Would they keep you safe and sound?
Wrapped up in eternal rainbows,
No chance of being found

Alas, I turned my back,
A reflection I could not see,
Young faces in the mirror,
I know this child is me.

CONTINUE LIFE

I sit underneath the old oak tree, acorns falling,
Watching squirrels collectively gather
In readiness for the chill of winter's ground frost,
Lost in the moment of nature, oblivious to the passing of time.
Trees change in season, leaves budding in spring, fresh and ready
To tantalise with colourful blossoms,
Into rapturous green on a summer's eve,
Autumn arrives as an array of orange hue,
Burning shades of deep red and gold in the crisp of cool air.
Winter comes quickly, a cold snap and suddenly,
The starkness of freezing days and dark nights swoop upon us

Life continues

No preparation, yet we know seasons change, year in, year out,
But are we ever prepared for a shift, from ourselves,
Through actions of others, or for the unexpected thrown upon us?
No matter what is echoing inside, however desperate we are
For time to stand still, to grasp onto one more minute,
Whether in slow motion or at hurried speed

Life continues

Not every individual is on a journey, a mission to find themselves,
But we all walk on the road that lies ahead,
Sometimes in quiet thought or in joyous steps
Each chapter not written for you to see, but for discovery,
Our hearts may desire to know the end of the story,
But hidden beauty can be found on the way there

Continue life.

TWO DOORS DOWN

Two doors down, lived the child no one knew,
Who played quietly inside,
With her eyes downcast on the squiggled lines of the hallway rug.
Every now and then, she would glance up,
To see an upside-down home crumbling slowly
Into faded patterns hard to distinguish,
Neighbours thought they witnessed the complete and whole,
A smiling heart and outstretched arms,
But how could they see beyond lines of recognition,
Only visible to the breath of an unknown sigh?

Time passed by
And two doors down, lived the grown-up no one knew,
Whose heart beat in unknown silence,
Echoing hollow and empty within,
Sounds of smashing plates tapping feverishly in the mind,
Disappearing in a vortex of swirling red mist.
Yet each day, she waved to the postman who wasn't there
And fulfilled her whispered promise to show up to work,
A pasted smile, for those who couldn't see
And as the day came and left,
So too did the adult, no one knew

Until such time when she knew.

Two doors down, lived the lady everyone knew,
Whose name carried far and wide
With stories to tell, gathering strength in number.
Listen carefully, you may recognise her voice
In her life,
In your life.
Be ready to embrace her into tomorrow's light,
For you never know who lives two doors down.

APPROVAL AND ACCEPTANCE

It begins without knowledge of entering humanity,
A baby passed between family and friends, the cooing and praise,
The worry from parents.
Does my baby meet with approval?
And so, it continues.

The child who seeks a smile from a parent,
Trying hard to win attention from a teacher,
The admiration from your first crush
Into adulthood, the new job, working to impress your boss,
A future partner,
From others unaware of who you are, your thoughts,
Your feelings intermingled with social media
And still the same desire

For approval or is it for acceptance?
Ingrained into human nature,
Even the animal kingdom,
The peacock who struts around
Displaying its beauty for all to see and admire.

But do we ever question
When it goes beyond the carefully drawn lines?
Has it always been there, indoctrinated from early life,
Or learnt as time goes on?
For the child who lives within disapproving walls,
Wishing for a snippet of approval just once,
For the teenager changing her appearance to blend in with the rest,
Too scared to stand out,

For the adult existing in a hushed relationship, seeking approval.
Acceptance and approval,
Closely interwoven,
Whether growing up under the sanctity of a harmonious background
Or the mercy of harm's way,
It remains.

Approval,
Acceptance,
Who is it for?
For you?
For family?
For friends?
For everyone else?

At times it could be just what is required
To flourish under guidance,
But when toxicity of damage is too great a cost,
Trying to conform to expectation,
Realisation sets in
On a road that may be hard to travel.
Give yourself permission to be good enough,
Live your life for you.

REPLENISHED WATERFALL

Do I have to come crashing down to find a way back,
Or can strength arise deep within?
Daydream wishes to shout from the rooftop,
Hear me now
Take heed
Whether I sing to release fluttered wings
Or cascading roars to replenish the waterfall.

I own my voice
I have the key
I can only ever be me.
Open the gates
Fling far and wide
Walk through with courage, head held up high.
I will only ever be me
I make the choice to set myself free.

I STAND STRONG

Past and present, as much as I try,
Permeates beyond the boundaries of existence,
Disguised in a pounding heart, in creeping shadows
As tiny conversations with my mind.
A reminder on each shoulder,
One for the day, another for the night,
But for each thorn that hurts
And every poisoned arrow,
Ready to strike from the mouth of the serpent,
I stand strong.

In my pain,
Through my strength,
With shared wisdom,
Embraced in love.

My tears have swum to the depths of the ocean and found their way back to shore,
An elixir of joy,
My scars are an invisible pattern etched deep inside,
Only I can see

Until now

Where I share my wounds with the world outside,
Not for a sticking plaster, a temporary fix,
But a chance to repair, time to heal.
Dressed in new attire,
Shining bright as a star,
Proud and worthy to sparkle,
A voice ready to flourish in a different landscape
In the presence of fear, through the dawn of a new awakening,
I stand strong.

BREAKING THE CHAINS

I cannot undo the broken shadows,
Or fix a crooked path,
Wipe away residue of pain left behind,
Change the time that was.
But I shall sing my song,
The voice inside of me,
Of ending years in silence,
Breaking chains to set you free.

I may falter on the journey
In moments of doubt, to cope,
With perseverance and faith inside,
I know there is always hope.
But I shall sing my song,
The voice inside of me,
Of ending years in silence,
Breaking chains to set you free.

I'm not naïve to the wounded soldiers,
Fragmented shards pierced in sorrow,
Wishes for peace and harmony,
A new day for a brighter tomorrow.
But I shall sing my song,
The voice inside of me,
Of ending years in silence,
Breaking chains to set you free.

I listen to the cries of the heart,
Each story is worthy to share,
Fragility needs to be nurtured,
Each layer, given chance to repair.
But I shall sing my song,
The voice inside of me,
Of ending years in silence,
Breaking chains to set you free.

I have not forgotten the past,
Of trauma, loss, the fear we repress,
Calmness and tranquillity, a challenge to acquire
For those, whose lives are shrouded with stress.
But I shall sing my song,
The voice inside of me,
Of ending years in silence,
Breaking chains to set you free.

I am learning new lessons, gathering strength
To awaken the fire, and smile inside
In trepidation, yet a road I must travel,
For we all are warriors, not willing to hide.
But I shall sing my song,
The voice inside of me,
Of ending years in silence,
Breaking chains to set you free.

I seek change in an ever-evolving landscape,
Uncertainty can confuse clarity in mind,
Imagine, just picture, civilisation with compassion
I believe, exists through the soul of our kind.
But I shall sing my song,
The voice inside of me,
Of ending years in silence,
Breaking chains to set you free.

www.ingramcontent.com/pod-product-compliance
Lightning Source LLC
Chambersburg PA
CBHW060228050426
42446CB00013B/3221